MW01267603

CRIME LAB DETECTIVES

John Townsend

amicus

Published by Amicus
P.O. Box 1329
Mankato, MN 56002

Printed in the United States of America at Corporate Graphics, in North Mankato, Minnesota.

Library of Congress Cataloging-in-Publication Data
Townsend, John, 1955-
  Crime lab detectives / John Townsend.
      p. cm. -- (Amazing crime scene science)
  Includes index.
  Summary: "Describes the types of items found at a crime scene that can be pieces of evidence
  in a criminal investigation, such as hair and saliva that carry DNA, fingerprints, clothing fibers,
  and foot prints. Includes real case files and case studies"--Provided by publisher.
  ISBN 978-1-60753-170-8 (library binding)
  1. Crime scene searches--Juvenile literature. 2. Evidence, Criminal--Juvenile literature.
  3. Criminal investigation--Juvenile literature. 4. Forensic sciences--Juvenile literature. I. Title.
  HV8073.8.T676 2012
  363.25--dc22

                                     2010044370

Appleseed Editions, Ltd.
Created by Q2AMedia
Editor: Katie Dicker
Art Director: Harleen Mehta
Designer: Neha Kaul
Picture Researcher: Debabrata Sen

All words in **bold** can be found in the Glossary on pages 30–31.

Picture credits
t= top, b= bottom, l= left, r= right

Leah Anne Thompson/Shutterstock: Title page, Kraska/Shutterstock: Contents page, Peter Menzel/Science Photo Library: 4,
Denis Closon/Rex Features: 5, United National Photographers/Rex Features: 6, Mason Morfit/The Medical File/
Photolibrary: 7, Jonathan Parry/Istockphoto: 8, Vladm/Shutterstock, Dc Slim/Shutterstock, Anthony Redpath/Corbis: 9t,
Shutterstock: 9c, Thumb/Shutterstock: 9b, Leah Anne Thompson/Shutterstock: 10, Corepics/Shutterstock: 11, George Musil,
Visuals Unlimited/Science Photo Library: 12, Mark St George/Rex Features: 13, Rex Features: 14, Steve Gschmeissner/
Science Photo Library: 15, Bruno Morandi/Photolibrary: 16, Undergroundarts.co.uk/Shutterstock: 17t, Derek Henthorn/
Photolibrary: 17b, Shevelev Vladimir/Shutterstock: 18, Mauro Fermariello/Science Photo Library: 19, Steger Volker/Photolibrary:
20, Mauro Fermariello/Science Photo Library: 21, Philippepsaila/Science Photo Library: 22, Fritz Reiss/
AP Photo: 23t, Library of Congress: 23cr, Maciej Medynski/Shutterstock: 24, Monalyn Gracia/Photolibrary: 25,
Paul Sancya/AP Photo: 26, Michael Donne, University Of Manchester/Science Photo Library: 27,
Daniel Berehulak/Getty Images: 28, Volker Steger/Photolibrary: 29, Jonathan Parry/Istockphoto: 31.
Cover image: Leah-Anne Thompson/Shutterstock.

DAD0052
3-2011

9 8 7 6 5 4 3 2 1

CONTENTS

The Crime Lab

Crime scenes can contain hundreds of pieces of **evidence**. The **CSI** team must find, collect, seal, and label each piece before sending it to the crime laboratory—where some amazing science awaits.

Crime Scientists

A lot of detective work occurs in crime laboratories (or **forensic** labs). The latest equipment helps crime scientists study the evidence from crime scenes. Strict rules are followed to ensure no piece of evidence is altered. Tests also have to be accurate because the results may be used in **court**.

This Federal Bureau of Investigation (FBI) laboratory in Washington, DC, tests bodily fluids found at crime scenes.

Different Tests

Each area of a crime laboratory specializes in different types of forensic science, including fingerprints, blood, glass fragments, hair and fibers, firearms, bones, handwriting, and footprints.

Every piece of evidence may need to be tested many times. A gun used in a robbery, for example, might be tested for fingerprints and then examined by a blood expert and a **ballistics** specialist.

This book explains some of the evidence crime lab detectives study to determine what happened during a crime. You may be surprised by some of their amazing crime science.

DID YOU KNOW?

Records of who is responsible for each piece of evidence—from the time it is found at the crime scene to each test in the lab—is called "the chain of **custody**." These records are necessary to make sure the evidence is kept in perfect condition.

A forensic scientist collects evidence, such as skin particles or blood, from a handgun.

Body Secrets

One of the great developments in crime lab science is **DNA** testing. What exactly is DNA and what happens in the lab to a DNA sample?

A Unique Code

DNA is a chemical in all of our billions of body **cells**. It is like a code locked in our **genes**. Everyone's DNA is different—except for some identical twins.

Cells in hair, dandruff, blood, saliva, or body tissue found at a crime scene can help to prove if a **suspect** was near the incident. Sweat usually contains dead skin cells and these cells are useful for forensic scientists to test. Nervous criminals often sweat a lot! Their DNA can be checked in the lab and matched against police records. If there is an exact match to a known criminal, the police will know who to find.

A scientist takes a sample of dried blood from some fabric for DNA testing.

DNA Patterns

By making a DNA **profile**, a forensic scientist can compare DNA found at a crime scene with a sample from a suspect. A method to profile DNA was discovered in 1984. The technique has developed since then. By using particular chemicals and electrical equipment, a DNA sample (taken from saliva inside the cheek, for example) can be made into a pattern on a sheet of film. If two different DNA samples match, they probably came from the same person.

A DNA profile can be compared to a police database to see if it matches any known criminals.

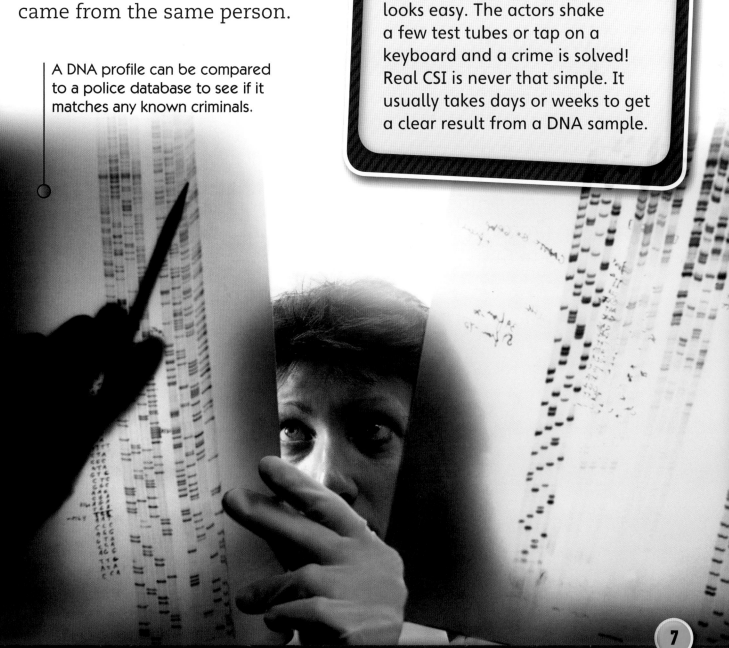

DID YOU KNOW?

In television crime dramas, the science in the crime lab often looks easy. The actors shake a few test tubes or tap on a keyboard and a crime is solved! Real CSI is never that simple. It usually takes days or weeks to get a clear result from a DNA sample.

Criminal Mouths

Many criminals have been caught because they failed to keep their mouths closed at a crime scene. A single drop of spit is enough for the crime lab to identify a suspect.

Telltale Saliva

Scientists can extract DNA from a tiny amount of saliva taken on a **swab** from a surface at the crime scene or on a criminal's discarded cigarette, apple core, or gum. The scientists then study the DNA profile of the person they need to find.

SCIENCE SECRETS

Saliva can give scientists more than a "spitting image" of a suspect. A single drop of saliva will soon allow scientists to tell from DNA evidence how healthy a person is and if they are likely to develop a life-threatening condition.

When a swab of saliva is taken from a suspect, the DNA can be compared to a sample found at the crime scene.

CASE FILE

In 2009, a bank robber from California left his mask behind at a bank he was robbing for a third time. He shot a gun at the ceiling and terrified the staff before running off with thousands of dollars. Crime lab detectives found saliva around the mask's opening for the mouth. They matched the DNA to Froilan Alix Roldan, a known criminal. In court, Roldan pleaded guilty to armed robbery and was sent to prison for 18 years.

Traces of saliva on a robber's dropped mask can lead to an arrest.

CASE FILE

In 2010, a New York burglar was sent to prison because of evidence he left behind when he raided a warehouse. Thirty-five-year-old Anthony Miola already had a criminal record when he stole valuable hunting rifles, shotguns, office equipment, and tools in 2009. A CSI officer found part of a cigarette at the crime scene and sent it to the crime lab to be tested. Scientists matched saliva on the cigarette to Miola's DNA. He was quickly arrested and charged with the crime.

Blood Science

Crime scientists who study blood can find all kinds of information in the lab from blood spots and very old bloodstains to almost invisible blood specks.

Solving Mysteries

For many years, blood samples have revealed secrets in the crime lab. At first, scientists were only able to tell if the blood came from an animal or a human and whether it was from a known suspect. Blood science has a long history:

- 100 years ago, scientists could tell which of the four main blood groups a sample came from.

- In the 1950s, tests showed whether blood came from a male or a female.

- In the mid-1980s, DNA testing of blood samples began to be used in crime labs.

Bloodstain patterns can reveal the number of blows from a weapon or the different events in an attack.

Because of recent advances in DNA science, crime labs can now examine evidence from old, unsolved crimes and sometimes make amazing discoveries. Today, some prisoners are behind bars because new science has helped to **convict** them of crimes committed many years ago.

CASE FILE

In 1995, police in Jacksonville, Florida, found the murdered body of Patricia Hammond. She had been stabbed and a knife was found nearby. A trail of blood, thought to be the killer's, led away from the scene, but the crime lab could not match the DNA to any known criminal. When they ran tests again 14 years later, scientists matched the blood to Michael Chatman, who was in prison for burglary. He denied knowing the victim, but the crime lab had the evidence they needed.

The DNA found on a bloody weapon can help convict a killer.

Human Hair

Your hair can say a lot about you and your environment. Just one strand can reveal many secrets in a crime laboratory.

Hairy Clues

A hair root is made of living cells, which contain a good source of DNA. One complete hair, with its root intact, can provide a DNA profile and much more.

Chemicals in the bloodstream, such as drugs or poison, become absorbed in growing hair and are stored in the **follicles**. When scientists examine hair samples in the lab, they can find details of a person's diet as well as other substances that have affected the body. This area of forensic science is called **toxicology**. It helps determine how chemicals within a human body might have contributed to a crime.

Human hairs vary in color, but forensic tests reveal even more clues.

CASE FILE

In 2008, nine-year-old Shannon Matthews disappeared from her home in Yorkshire, UK. Her mother appeared on television to plead for her safe return, and newspapers offered a large reward.

More than 250 police officers and 60 detectives worked on the investigation. After nearly a month, they found Shannon imprisoned in a house belonging to Michael Donovan—the mother's boyfriend. Donovan and Shannon's mother had planned the kidnapping to get the reward money. Instead, they were sent to prison for eight years.

One of the key pieces of evidence at the trial was Shannon's hair, which showed that Shannon had been given different drugs over many weeks to keep her sleepy, even before she was kidnapped. Donovan possessed the same drugs. The proof was overwhelming.

Tests on strands of Shannon's hair revealed details about her kidnapping.

DID YOU KNOW?

Head hair grows about 0.39 to 0.59 inches (1 to 1.5 cm) a month. Tests on different parts of a hair can identify when a substance was absorbed by the body. One hair can determine race, gender, drugs, vitamin deficiencies, and if the hair fell out naturally, was pulled out, or was cut.

Dog Hairs and DNA

Sometimes, forensic scientists have used the DNA from a pet to help solve a crime. Although it's not a foolproof method, pets can help to provide vital evidence.

The Murder of Leanne Tiernan

In 2001, a man walking his dog in the woods in Yorkshire, UK, found the body of 16-year-old Leanne Tiernan 10 miles (16 km) from her home. She had been missing for nine months. Fingerprints, DNA, and clothing helped to identify her body. The **pathologist** said Leanne had been strangled and that her body was stored somewhere cool before being taken to the woods.

A black plastic bag over Leanne's head was tied with a dog collar, a scarf, and a cable around her neck. Leanne's murderer then wrapped her body in green plastic trash liners and tied it with twine.

The police discovered that John Taylor had bought dog collars locally and had been seen in the same woods. When the police searched Taylor's house, they found more cable and an identical dog collar.

Leanne Tiernan (right) with her sister shortly before her tragic murder

This is what dog hairs look like under a microscope.

Scientists found a strand of pink carpet fiber on Leanne's sweater. Even though Taylor had burned his carpet, CSI officers found strands of pink fiber on a nail at Taylor's house. The fibers matched the strand on Leanne's clothing.

DNA Clues

Scientists tested items found near Leanne's body, including the scarf tied around her neck. The knot contained a small amount of Taylor's DNA in a human hair and dog hairs were on Leanne's body. However, because Taylor's dog had recently died, the DNA results could not be used as evidence in court.

CSI officers then searched under floorboards at Taylor's house and found bloodstains. Scientists were able to prove that the blood DNA matched Leanne's. In 2002, John Taylor was sentenced to prison for life.

Dog Evidence

Sometimes dogs have helped solve crimes by accident. What they have left behind at crime scenes can be bagged up and taken to the lab as vital evidence.

Dog DNA

Just like humans, all dogs have **unique** DNA. But it's not just dog hairs found at crime scenes or on suspects that have linked a specific animal to a particular criminal. Sometimes, the evidence has caused a fuss and created quite a stink!

CASE FILE

In 1999, a man attacked a woman in her yard in Iowa. Crime lab scientists used her dog's urine to catch the criminal. The woman was unable to identify her attacker in a **police lineup**, but she remembered his car and that her dog had urinated on one of the tires.

A urine sample was taken from the suspect's car and tested in a crime lab. When scientists confirmed it came from the victim's dog, it was all the evidence they needed to put the attacker behind bars for two years.

A dog's urine can help to catch a criminal if it is found on important evidence.

CASE FILE

Dog feces on an armed bank robber's shoe in Gold Coast, Australia, in 2000 landed him right in it! Twenty-six-year-old Jacob Smith walked around a bank he was robbing before he ran off. CSI officers had the job of sniffing out his smelly footprints. "It's the first time I've ever got a pattern left by dog poo," the forensic officer said.

When Smith was arrested, it was just a matter of matching his shoe to the shoe print at the crime scene. Then the feces was tested with deposits stuck on his shoe—a perfect match! Smith was sentenced to nearly 11 years in prison for robbery.

Shoe evidence can be used to track the movements of a crime suspect.

SCIENCE SECRETS

In 2002, David Westerfield kidnapped and murdered seven-year-old Danielle van Dam in California. CSI officers found dog hairs at his home even though he had no pets. The hairs had come from Danielle's clothes. By comparing the hair samples to Danielle's dog, scientists found a DNA match. This evidence helped to convict Westerfield of murder.

Microscopic Images

By using the latest microscopes and **infrared** technology, crime labs can examine glass fragments, soil, or paint in the closest detail.

Broken Glass

Criminals often break into property by smashing a window. The shower of tiny glass fragments can help to catch the criminal. Glass dust and splinters stick to clothing or get trapped in folds or pockets. If these pieces of glass match the glass from a crime scene, it can be used as vital evidence.

A light microscope can show if two tiny fragments are from the same pane of glass. A chemical test can also reveal whether two glass samples were made in exactly the same way.

Glass fragments from a crime scene can be matched to samples found on a suspect.

Finding a Match

Sometimes, forensic scientists need to test a speck of paint, a tiny fiber, or a grain of soil. The victim of a hit-and-run attack, for example, may have a chip of paint left on their clothing from a particular make and model of car. Scientists may match fibers or mud found on a victim's body to those from a suspect's clothing, furniture, or carpet.

A **spectrometer** examines and measures how a sample of soil, paint, or fiber absorbs infrared light. This can prove exactly where the sample came from.

A forensic scientist uses a spectrometer to identify whether samples are linked to a crime scene.

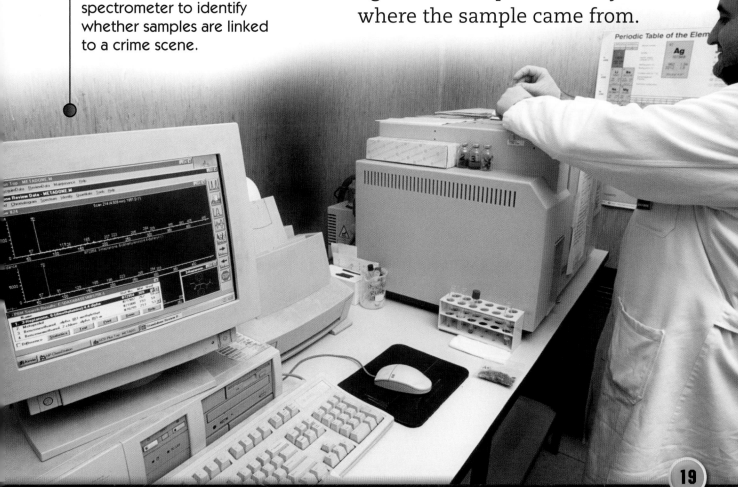

Fiber Proof

Crime labs test many clothing samples. Fabric and fibers found on victims and suspects can hold many secrets that scientists can uncover.

Clothes in the Lab

Clothing and footwear often contain evidence—from stains, labels, and unique fibers to a sprinkle of skin cells full of DNA or tiny **pollen** grains. Much of forensic science involves testing tiny threads and dyes found in clothing and items stuck to them. These tests can prove if someone was at a crime scene.

This forensic scientist uses tape to collect fibers from a clothing sample for further testing.

CASE FILE

In 2001, UK police found the murdered body of 54-year-old Michael Reaney in the bedroom of his London home, which had been robbed. CSI officers gathered many pieces of evidence, including fibers, hairs, and fabric. The police watched two suspects—Francis Carbon and Andrew Docherty—who were soon arrested during a robbery.

Crime lab detectives found links between the two robbers and Reaney's murder. Fibers found on tape stuck around Michael's face matched those on gloves worn by Carbon. Tests on other items from the murder scene proved that Carbon and Docherty were the killers. This evidence put them behind bars.

DID YOU KNOW?

The soles of shoes can reveal clues in a crime lab. Just like fingerprints, no two shoe prints are exactly the same. Footwear gets marked by sharp objects or can wear away in distinct patches. Cuts or tiny stones in the tread leave telltale marks that crime lab detectives can identify.

Fibers from a crime scene can be compared to fibers taken from a suspect.

Paper Crime

Crime labs often examine documents and test if they are genuine or **forgeries**. What might seem like a real letter or suicide note sometimes can be proved to be a fake.

Fake Documents

Many criminals have tried to make or alter documents for all kinds of reasons—usually money. But changing a handwritten or typed page can be detected when scientists use **ultraviolet**, infrared, or laser light, which makes newer ink glow differently.

Forensic **graphology** experts specialize in handwriting and can determine whose writing it is and whether it is genuine. This is useful when the police examine **ransom** notes, threatening letters, or **blackmail** demands.

Fingerprints don't normally show up on paper. The chemical DFO reacts with sweat to reveal fingerprints under an ultraviolet light.

SCIENCE SECRETS

Crime labs use ESDA (Electrostatic Detection Apparatus) tests to reveal evidence on paper that is invisible to the naked eye. The test can show traces of fingerprints and whether a document has been altered.

CASE FILE

In 1979, the Hitler Diaries became world news. A German magazine learned that diaries had been found, which had been written by the leader of Germany in World War II, Adolf Hitler (1889–1945). Such documents would be worth a fortune.

An extract from the Hitler Diaries discovered in 1979

Adolf Hitler

It seemed the diaries had survived after a plane carrying Hitler's papers crashed at the end of World War II. A great deal of money was paid for the diaries—but then people began to question if they were genuine. Forensic scientists studied the handwriting as well as the paper, ink, and diary covers. Some interesting discoveries were made:

- The paper contained chemicals that were not used in papermaking until about 10 years after Hitler's death.

- Threads binding the diaries contained fibers that were not available when Hitler was alive.

- Tests on the ink proved the diaries had been written only recently.

It was clear that the Hitler Diaries were fakes. The forger, Konrad Kujau, was sentenced to four and a half years of prison for forgery in 1985.

Forensic Images

Our images are often captured by **CCTV** cameras. Any criminal activity they record may go to the crime lab and forensic experts.

Videos in the Lab

With cameras pointing at us in buildings and on the streets, many crimes are now caught on video. But the image quality is often poor and the police have difficulty identifying suspects. Forensic experts use computer software to improve the video clips and forensic imaging techniques to study each frame. The digital material is run through software to sharpen the pictures, highlight important areas, and print quality video stills.

Closed-circuit television (CCTV) cameras can help to trace a criminal's movements.

Jean Prints

Forensic scientists can use forensic imaging to enlarge patterns in the fibers of fabric. Jeans, in particular, have hidden patterns. Images can zoom in on a suspect's jeans and measure details of seams and woven threads. The crime lab can make an image map of these features, wrinkles, and tucks. The information is **digitized**, much like a fingerprint, and is used to match jeans found in the home of a suspect.

CASE FILE

As early as 1996, the Federal Bureau of Investigation (FBI) identified a bank robber by his jeans on a security video. Even though he wore a mask to hide his face, the robber of the Spokane Bank in Washington was caught. The crime lab zoomed in on worn patches on his jeans showing distinct patterns. A suspect's jeans had more than 24 features that matched the jean's "barcode," and he was convicted of the crime.

DID YOU KNOW?

Video images recorded at crime scenes can produce face prints that can be matched to a digital image of a suspect's face. By measuring the spaces and angles between key points on a face, scientists can find a match with face prints of known criminals. Our face prints, like our fingerprints, are unique.

A robber may run from a scene, but images of his jeans could help to catch him.

Face Secrets

In some crime labs, forensic scientists work with human bones and skulls to piece together vital clues. So what do they actually do?

Making Faces

If a human skeleton is discovered, experts may need to study it in the lab to identify the person, the cause of death, and the killer. Sometimes, the only way to identify a victim is to find out what the dead person looked like. By reconstructing the face from clay, using a plaster cast model of the skull, it is possible to jog memories of anyone who knew the person.

This forensic pathologist works on a model of a person's face to help identify the victim.

Latest Technology

Another way of reconstructing the face is to measure key parts of the skull and create a face map with a computer. A laser scans the skull. A computer then calculates exact details and measurements to add layers of muscle, tissue, and lifelike skin. The computer image can be rotated to show how the unidentified person once looked from all angles.

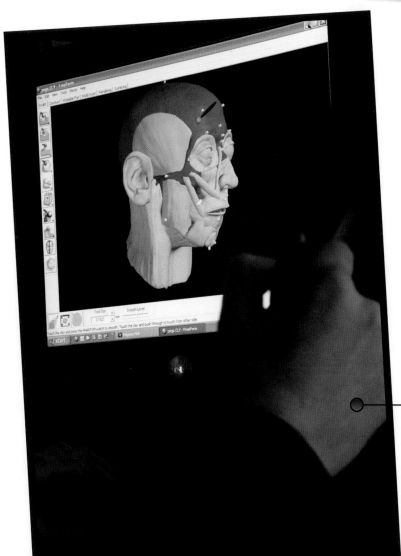

A finished image is then compared to a missing persons' database to see if there are any matches. If not, the police may send the image to newspapers and television stations. Many human remains have been identified in this way.

Forensic scientists use computers to reconstruct the features of a face.

27

What Next?

New crime scene science and the latest developments in crime labs will make future forensic work even more amazing. What will crime labs come up with next?

Mobile Crime Labs

Some police departments are developing high-tech vehicles with onboard crime labs so that a small laboratory can be quickly set up at the crime scene. These labs will speed up forensic testing.

Many mobile labs carry the latest equipment, including:
- scanning electron microscopes (SEM), which are ideal for recording high-quality digital images at a crime scene;
- handheld lights that reveal fingerprints as well as blood, sweat, shoe prints, human bone fragments, drugs, and chemicals;
- 3D microscopes for measuring and comparing marks on fired bullets to prove if a gun was fired at a crime scene; and
- handheld DNA detectors for quicker forensic testing.

Mobile labs help speed up investigations and reduce the risk of evidence being tainted.

More Forensic Images

Crime labs continue to develop **biometric** equipment to measure a suspect's facial features, hand measurements, body odor, and tone of voice. Scans can also give a printout of the eye or even the brain.

Face-recognition technology can identify criminals caught on camera. Linked to a database that stores criminal records, this technology may soon allow police officers to get instant information on a suspect. Forensic science is always on the move!

CAN YOU BELIEVE IT?

Face-recognition technology can identify people even if they age or change their looks. The University of Miami has developed a system of photographing someone's face and ears and comparing the results with prestored images of the same person. It is almost 100 percent accurate.

A person's face can be scanned onto a computer and checked against police records.

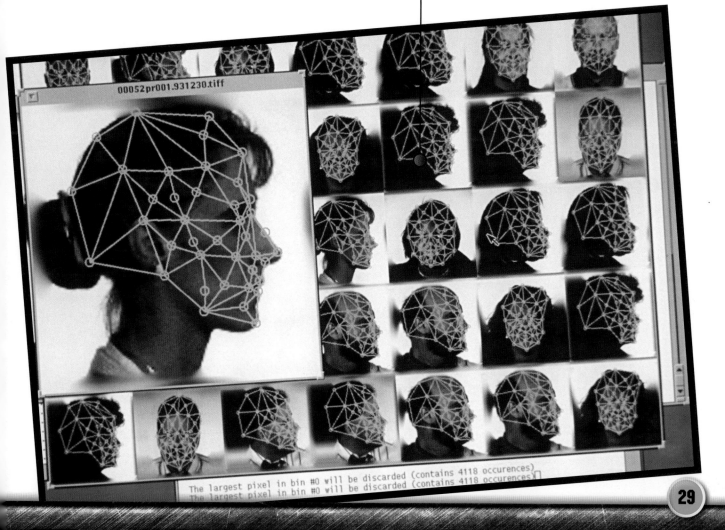

00052pr001.931230.tiff

The largest pixel in bin #0 will be discarded (contains 4118 occurences)
The largest pixel in bin #0 will be discarded (contains 4118 occurences)

Glossary

ballistics
the science of the motion of objects (such as bullets) that are fired

biometric
the study of measurable biological characteristics, particularly of the face and body

blackmail
trying to force a person to do or pay something by threatening to reveal a secret

CCTV
closed-circuit television

cells
the basic building blocks of all living things, which are continually being renewed

convict
to prove someone guilty of a crime in court

court
the place where a criminal is questioned and proven innocent or guilty

CSI
crime scene investigation

custody
keeping safe and secure

digitized
to change images, text, or sound into digital form for use by a computer

DNA
the code in each person's cells that makes everyone unique

evidence
material presented to a court to prove the truth in a crime case

follicle
a small cavity in the skin that contains cells for growing hair

forensic
using scientific methods to investigate and establish facts in criminal courts

forgery
a fake copy of something with the aim of passing it off as real

genes
sets of instructions in all our body cells that make us who we are

graphology
the study of handwriting to discover a writer's personality or identity

infrared
energy waves (radiation) that can be used to show and measure usually invisible details

innocent
not guilty of a crime

pathologist
a forensic scientist who examines samples of body tissue and dead bodies

police lineup
an identity parade where a witness tries to recognize a suspect

pollen
the powder found inside flowers, which helps plants reproduce

profile
a set of results often in the form of a graph that shows key characteristics

ransom
something paid or demanded for the freedom of a captured person

refractive
the bending of light rays that pass at an angle through different objects

spectrometer
a tool used to split light waves into their different colors

suspect
someone thought to be guilty of a crime

swab
a cotton bud on a stick used for taking a sample of saliva or sweat

toxicology
the study of harmful effects of chemical and physical substances on living things

ultraviolet
light that can reveal blood and fingerprints that are not visible to the naked eye

unique
only one like it in the entire world

Index

Web Finder

www.all-about-forensic-science.com/forensic-science-video.html
Learn all about forensic science from DNA to toxicology.

http://encyclopedia.kids.net.au/page/fo/Forensics
Discover more about forensic techniques from the study of insects and pollen to canines and computers.

www.howstuffworks.com/biometrics.htm
Learn more about the study of biometrics.

www.sciencenewsforkids.org/articles/20060201/Feature1.asp
Learn what forensic scientists can tell from a swab of saliva.

www.sciencenewsforkids.org/articles/20080305/Note2.asp
Find out how your hair can reveal a lot about who you are.